Listening

Listening

Dr. Thelma Bowles

1663 Liberty Drive

Bloomington, IN 47403

Order this book online at www.trafford.com
or email orders@trafford.com

Most Trafford titles are also available at major online book retailers.

Printed in the United States of America.

ISBN: 978-1-4269-4845-9 (sc)

Trafford rev. 11/08/2010

 www.trafford.com

North America & international
toll-free: 1 888 232 4444 (USA & Canada)
phone: 250 383 6864 ♦ fax: 812 355 4082

To the memory of Hazel Bowman, a teacher of the
importance of listening

Preface

After a lifetime of learning and many years in educational settings, it has become clear that I have done a lot of listening. In an attempt to make some sense of how such listening has affected and effected my quality of life, I determined to venture into the domain of print listening, that is, I began to assemble my understanding of listening and as it impacts life. You have been invited into this domain from my perspective with your own perspectives in tow. Perhaps, hopefully, you will become revitalized through this excursion.

Introduction

There is more to listening than the auditory end-result of that which we know as hearing. The concept, to listen, pervades all aspects of the myriad interactions on earth. In order to view listening from this mindset, you are asked to:

…"take several giant-steps backward, please"…

After a brief description of the commonly recognized function of what man understands to be to listen, auditory hearing; listening will be viewed as it is accomplished by a single-celled and a lower life-form. Several other life- and physical-forms of listening will be scattered throughout the text. Having 'listened' as understood by other forms in the near cosmos, you will make the determination or your reorientation with respect to that which you consider to be the appropriate human position for you as one in the vast and interconnected cosmos.

Further human listening, with the focus on all the senses will be viewed at varying depths. And, finally, you will be challenged to rethink your understandings with respect to 'listen'.

Succinctly put, the format is a simple one – you have been given a general overview of what you will be told regarding listening. Next, you will be told what it means to listen along with some examples of listening. And, finally, you will be told what you were told. Simply put, you will delve into the art and science of listening at various levels and depths several times. Such reinforced and clarifications surrounding listening, a technique used to internalize information has been used for eons and has proven very successful.

Finally, in answer to your question: 'Yes', it is worth the energy. The path, though well trodden, will be fresh, and your ability to listen will be enriched exponentially. You will be rewarded for making the decision to use your energy in this endeavor.

The Nature and Use of this Book

Effective listening is that which is viewed from many personal and interpersonal venues. The act of and intention to listen is a complex process, one that has been studied by many people in an effort to acquire a better understanding of the process. It has been studied, addressed, and expounded upon by sources as divergent as scholars, politicians, songwriters, parents, and (probably) many of your friends and enemies. Some of those definitions or views of listening will be exposed for their measure of truth, while others may simply be presented as they relate to the broad subject of listening. They may represent areas, if you so choose, for further study.

Finally, a few sources of a biological, ecological, and social nature are referenced for more in depth listening from those perspectives. As indicated in the first part of the introduction above, listening is a broad and well traveled concept. The attempt to cover it completely in this one source would be presumptuous. A small and incomplete documentation of what it means to listen, along with examples and references to other sources for more about listening is the nature of this book.

TABLE OF CONTENTS

Listening:

The sum total of (a) recognition of a message or messages, and (b) the reaction to the message(s) based on (c) the accumulated previous messages and reactions

Chapter One – Early Listening

Humans have listened for thousands of years. The aspect of a distant relative to present day humans, Cro-Magnon man, explains the importance of listening clearly. That very important aspect is that the species no-longer exists.

Cro-Magnon man existed thousands of years before the current species known as Homo sapiens. The fact that the species called Cro-Magnon no longer exists has everything to do with the importance of listening. Listening to the surroundings: the air, the predators, the evolutionary plant and chemical messages; was and continues to be necessary in the current species of man, as well as for all living things, for continued existence. Unfortunately, sometimes that is not enough as evolution demonstrates.

Organisms genetically unable to survive the changing environment, that is, unable to effectively listen to the cues provided by all components of their surroundings and to respond in a timely manner, remove themselves from the mix at various stages in the process of species refinement. This redefining process has occurred from the beginning of existence and continues to occur in all living things today.

Listening is extremely complex and, yet, very basic by nature. The concept is biological, social, and evolutionary, bringing the 'nature versus nurture' debate into glaring focus. As simple exercises in listening, the nature of existence of the single celled amoeba, the coral, and the honey bee and the red ant will be viewed directly. The extent of their success, as it regards listening for perpetuation of the species, will be brought to light.

A more complex listening, that interpreted by the humans, will be compared to that of these simple forms of life and with other mammals, along with examples of listenings and the totality of listening as an exercise for the perpetuation of life forms.

Chapter Two – Single-celled and Simple Organisms – an Exercise in Listening for Survival

Single-celled and simple organism existence may be a very accurate representation for all life. Such existence is that of symbiotic relationship between and among their various and varied parts and in orchestration with the surrounding environment, much like a symphony. The amoeba, sea sponges, and honey bee and red ant are examples of such symbiosis.

While the complexity of existence occupies the thoughts and consumes energies of many humans, simply existing is the extent of reality for other beings in the biological scene. This singularity, while very basic, accurately illustrates the nature of all existence. Some of these cells depend on listening for survival and put their future existence as well as that of any hosts in jeopardy when the nature of their listening is suspect or simply faulty. Others are content to exist in the environment in which they are found and to adjust, as required by the changes in the environments, to continue to coexist and to evolve. Simple and not so simple multi-celled organisms, similarly, impact their own existence as well as the existence of other living things by how effectively they listen to their many internal and external environments.

Amoeba

The amoeba is an example of an attuned single-celled life. Identified in the 1700s, the amoeba is a combination of compatible units. Working together for the common good, the external membrane and nucleus represent the major components of this being. The membrane keeps adversity out of the cell while holding all of the cellular components together. The nucleus has the responsibility for the major operation of continued and continuing existence. While both are important, without the other parts of the amoeba, it would not exist. This symbiotic relationship, this listening, between and among its various and varied parts define is single-celled creature.

The amoeba consists, in addition to the exterior membrane and the nucleus, of mitochondria, vacuoles, and intracellular fluid. The vacuole appears to be a useless thing taking up space in this small cell. It is, however, a vital component in the amoeba's immediate survival. The foremost function of the vacuole is as an adjustor to the acidity of the cell when the environment requires such adjustment. It may also be used, when needed, to clear the cell of unneeded matter. Thirdly, the vacuole is used to stabilize the cell in an often turbulent and congested area. Other parts of the cell, including those within the nucleus, have similar functions that benefit the whole. Due to the internal harmony between its various parts, the amoeba makes adjustments when required by the environment in which it is found and continues to exist as a species.

Sea Sponge

The classification known as sponges is very broad. The location of the habitat of the sponge and the structure of the sponge work in harmony.

Is the current swift? Then the sponge must be of the type that is able to bend and not break.

Is the body of water a salty sea? If the water is too salty, the outer membranes of the sponge must prevent the salty solution from compromising the organism such that the membrane is ruptured and the organism, thereby, destroyed.

Is the sponge blue or red or yellow or green? The color of the sponge is caused by the nutrition it consumes and the need to blend in with the environment for individual and species preservation.

You know that soft brown sponge your grandfather used to use to wash his car? That once was a living thing a living sponge (unless grandpa used the synthetic sponges). Visualize the appearance of the sponge. It contains a series of convoluted openings, tunnels and dead ends. That sponge was affixed to part of the coral reef and allowed the sea water, with its many tasty creatures, to flow into those convenient openings. Many of the creatures and vegetation never made it out in their original form. They became nourishment for the sponge or remained in a symbiotic relationship with the sponge.

Other sponges resemble miniature smoke stacks or cacti. The external surface may have cilia to sweep the food into the mouth of the sponge or lethal appendages to stun the organisms that get too close and then to entangle the unfortunate sea life, until consumed, similar to the amoeba's method for acquiring food.

One method of reproduction for the sponge is asexual. A broken piece of sponge, of sufficient size and consisting of the necessary component cells, becomes a new organism. The current may carry it away from the original spot or it may attach close to the original organism. If nutrition is not sufficient for all the sponges, the weaker ones will die. That is the present state of many of the coral reefs – the environment is not 'right', either in quantity or consistency, for continued life. Contamination by man or change in temperature, again due to Homo sapiens' indifference to other life forms, is often the case for the dilemma in which the present day seas find themselves.

A second asexual means of reproduction results when cells collect and encapsulate at the surface of the host organism. In this position these encapsulated entities accumulate food until there is sufficient supply for them to exist independently at which point they break off and become independent sponges.

In sexual reproduction, the sponges, which are bi-sexual, may play either role. Using the currents and flagella, the sperm is collected into the 'female', where fertilization takes place. The young sponge is protected until it has reached the appropriate level of maturity, at which point it is purged back into the environment to continue developing to the adult stage.

Dr. Thelma Bowles

The Honey Bee and the Ant – Pheromones and the caste roles

The most successful animal, with respect to survival, is the insect ^{mound}. Their ability to adapt the surrounding in which they are found makes them annoying, to say the least, and it is well worth considering the manner through which they accomplish such a feat (how they listen). Bees and ants are two of the insects in the largest group, the social insects. They are so described because they have a distinct division of labor.

The proportion of each division to the whole is controlled by 'signal systems' or pheromones. These pheromones are chemicals which control the development of the young members of the species in order to maintain the appropriate ratios between the different castes to the whole. This assures the needs of the colony are met. The concept will be viewed through life cycle of the honey bee and that of the ant in their respective environments.

The Honey Bee

There are three main castes in the life cycle of the bee – the queen, the worker, and the drone. The queen bee is responsible for reproducing the larvae that will become the next generations of honey bee. She is fed the pheromones, mixtures of chemical substances that cause changes in the physiology and behavior, specific to her task, the task she efficiently accomplishes. In addition to carrying the larvae for the period of gestation, she may assist in making ready the 'nest', which may be a castoff from birds or some other species of vertebrate, and supplies it with the nutrition the developing larvae will need for successful development to the bee stage.

The early honey bees are female. They are smaller than the queen as a consequence of their pheromones received, and called worker bees because of their functions – gathering pollen and nectar, ensuring the appropriateness of the hive for incubation, and the mundane tasks of maintaining the temperature appropriate for the young bees, and listening to each other for the locations of adequate and appropriate nutrient sources for the entire colony. Their lives are hard and they are soon worn out and die.

Later hatchings contain both female and male bees. The females carry on the roles established by their worker status while the males are used to impregnate the queen's eggs, period. Valuable nutrients cannot be wasted on these 'non-worker', non-queen bees. The male bees are, therefore, exterminated when the colony has no further use for them. How pheromones are distributed for generating the male versus the female hatchling is unclear, but the effect is definite.

The large ratio of this familial colony is represented by the worker bees. The worker segment of bee species has no reproductive function and needs to be large in number relative to the whole colony due to the nature of its jobs. The nutrition they seek comes in the form of pollen obtained from the plant species specific to the requirements of the particular species to which the workers belong.

The new queen is 'crowned' and impregnated, in the proper season, as the old queen dies. The cycle of life and death and life continues.

This insect species listens to the various environments in which it is found to acquire the materials needed in performing its life experience and contributes to the regeneration of plant species by way of 'accidentally' transporting pollen during its efforts for survival.

The Ant

Ants live in colonies and communicate by touch and smell. Each ant colony begins with a single queen ant who has mated once with a male and stores the sperm to use throughout her reproductive life. Just like the colonies of bees, the sterile female worker ants have the responsibility for providing the food and security for the developing ants. The ant cycle is egg to grub to pupa to mature ant. The colony is efficient in its efforts as it listens to the environment to assure adequate food and prevent their total demise as a consequence of toxic substances or other forms of potential annihilation.

Chapter Three – How do we Know what we Know?

Having become familiar with a few simple organisms and their codependences for successful perpetuation it becomes clear that listening and adaptation are needed.

Evolution has refined the nature of listening and adaptation. This process of evolution, in the case of understanding Homo sapiens' reproductive nature, has been viewed by scientists with increasing comprehension of the facts of 'who we are' and how humans came to be. In 500 to 400 B. C. Hippocrates and those of like mind, believed Homo sapiens began as completely formed miniature humans within adult bodies, as active 'humors'. Between 384 and 322 B. C., individuals such as philosopher and naturalist Aristotle, espoused the concept that forming human life was the consequence of joining male essence and female menstrual blood. The 'essences' recognized as sperm and ovum joined to form the embryo which developed progressively into what is a sustainable life-form, Homo sapiens, according to the then recognized form of human reproduction.

Listening, that is the use of the newly invented microscope, allowed for a more accurate understanding of the components of the reproduction of the human species. The instruments refined from the original microscope have been used for a more definitive recognition of reproduction and beyond. Listening research has identified how genetic code is passed from one generation to succeeding generations. In addition, chromosomes; genes; and deoxyribonucleic acid (DNA), the hereditary material of humans and other organisms were recognized and their functions identified through the continued efforts by the human species to define themselves.

Evolution and Nature versus Nurture

That the beliefs of the religious establishment were at odds with biological findings, effectively cemented the controversy which rages today. That controversy known as 'nature versus nurture' attempts to clarify the origin of various characteristics of our species collectively and as individuals. Whether we have evolved from lower forms of life is the question that remains in the minds of many humans.

The names Charles Darwin (who first espoused the theory of natural selection that suggests only the strong survive) and Gregor Mendel (a geneticist) are familiar to many in this twenty-first century as forerunners to our present understanding of our biology – who we are and how we came to be 'who we are'.

Cultivation has led to new strains of species of plants and animals. The same concept of cultivation or evolution may be the means by which humans evolved into the species as it is known today. The way genetic information is transferred from one generation to the next; whether stored or expressed, or regulated or altered; causes the line between the evolutionists' and the geneticists' views of the early to current formations of life in the human species to become blurred.

One concept on which both schools of thought agree is that listening is critical as a means of survival and in order to thrive as living forms in the cosmos. On this point of agreement we shall proceed to what is meant by the term 'listening' and how it effects the continuation and transformation of the species known as Homo sapiens, or more commonly, man.

Chapter Four – Concept and Anatomy of Listening

Through an example, you will recognize listening. Consider the physics of a thunder storm.

There are a number of stages or segments to any storm – the incremental collating of the necessary components, the increase in intensity and interactions of those components to a climax, and, ultimately, the wind down or conclusion to the storm.

Specifically, listening is an array of events and component parts. In human listening, the first mechanism thought of is the human ear. Humans listen through the device which begins at the external orifice, the external ear. While this is an important part of hearing, much more is involved if listening is to occur. The external ear is the receiver of that to which the body 'listens'. That which is seen is just the beginning of a complex system which culminates with the brain. This listening process is called hearing and is made up of iterations as the listening system, the

17

auditory system, defines, refines, and redefines that which it hears.

To understand the processes of listening with the ear and the additional parts of the auditory system, consider the wind. What is wind? What does it have to do with listening?

> Consider: There is silence. Next, you hear a gentle breeze or the sound of a strong wind. You understand this to be the wind which precedes a storm. The breeze and the more forceful wind are identical with the exception of velocity. The winds are the changes in pressures that occur in nature as the natural environment attempts to maintain or to regain equilibrium. The silence is the state wherein the air is less dense or in a state of low pressure. Your history with wind has shown that 'a storm is coming'. The reality is that wind with more pressure is coming to fill the space, reacquire the balance, between the two states of pressure.

You listen and hear and understand the sounds of the wind. How did all this understanding come to be?

The ear and its complementary auditory components were affected by the physical experience of varying pressures from beginning to end. It heard, felt, the wind from its state of uniform pressure to the condition of low density or low pressure through to the high pressure and eventually to the balance in pressure. This hearing occurred in a continuum throughout the mechanism of the ear and as a consequence of another component, history.

The brain had received these messages before and stored them for your present use. You know the extent of the storm and whether there is need for you to take cover or if you can simply to enjoy the experience.

> Consider: There is a loud scream! Many responses to the scream occur in the person who hears the scream. The auditory recognition of this sound is the same as for the wind. The cause of the sound is the same, but the source is different. In addition, the human 'startle response' is initiated. The old 'fight or flight' concept whereby adrenaline is pumped into the muscles to prepare the body to meet its enemy, to fight it or, if more appropriate, to flee from the dangerous and potentially lethal situation, is immediately set in place. Based on the body interpretation of need, on sound recognition and history, a response is given to that which has been heard. 'Is someone in trouble or is someone just having fun?'

The structure, commonly recognized as the method by which humans hear, as stated previously, is the ear. While the devices found on both sides of the human head are known as ears, the reality is the visual skin (and the enclosed cartilage) is simply a part of the outer ear. The outer ear is a very important part of hearing, but only one part.

The outer ear has three main parts: the outer fleshy part which is named the pinna, the opening (the auditory meatus), and the bony structure which surrounds the meatus, named the concha because of its shell-like nature. The air in the auditory meatus of the outer ear is sheltered by the shell-like design and, when in a state of silence, is less dense than the air of the surrounding atmosphere. Silence is a rare state, however, as the environment is always attempting to equalize densities. Air is generally flowing in and bouncing around the auditory meatus, impacting its walls and the adjoining surface of the next portion of the hearing device, the middle ear. This bouncing around is what we know to be listening as the effects of the air move from the outer ear through the middle portion of the auditory system and beyond.

The outermost portion of the middle ear is the tympanic membrane, commonly called the ear drum. "Held in place by fibers and cartilage and situated in a bony groove just past the outer ear, the tympanic membrane is the lateral boundary of the large middle ear cavity, the tympanum" [Yost]. The tympanic membrane vibrates as a result of sound waves received from the outer ear. The complimentary components to the membrane are bony in nature. They, along with other bones in the head afford secondary vibrations, received from the external environment. These middle ear bones are the malleus, incus, and stapes. These bones receive vibrations through their tendon, ligament and muscle connections to the tympanic membrane in addition to the tympanic membrane directly. These vibrations are received by the final part of the ear, the inner ear.

The outer boundary of the inner ear is the bottom of the stapes, which looks like the bottom of a stirrup (thus the name stapes), and is held in place by ligaments. The inner ear is composed of fluid and thousands of neurons, receptors for the vibrations from the middle ear. Officially the inner ear is said to consist of semicircular canals, a vestibule, and the cochlea.

Interpretation of human hearing

Much has been written and presented about human listening. The following is one such presentation:

> Listening takes place through the apparatuses in the head; the physical, which has just been discussed; and the psychological which is represented by interpretations given to those synaptic firings of the complex of neurons in the brain and elsewhere in the body. The third and fourth components of listening and the comprehension thereof have to do with pitch, rhythm and phrasing. These components vary by language, culture, experience with the vibrations and with the personality of the individual receiving the message. Finally, the perception by the receiving individual, of the intent and credibility of the sender of the message/ vibrations impacts the recognition.[Charles]

The Nature of the Individual and Listening

There is obviously more to listening than the auditory connections. With that recognition in mind, take a look at the individual hearer in relation to his/ her personality.

The nature of the listener (the one who hears), is often identified through the answers given to a series of questions known as a 'personality type' inventory. One of those inventories is the Myers-Briggs Personality Inventory MBTI® which recently has been revised by the publisher to allow for on-line administration and interpretation. In this inventory there are sixteen possible personality types. When individuals are interacting with others, the personality types have an impact on the listening, what is the supposed meaning of the communication, and the responses as a result of the presumed meanings transmitted and received. Many lost friendships have resulted from faulty listening or, at least, misinterpretation of the message.

A similar inventory is known as the Cognitive Style Inventory©. The most recent revision of this personality type descriptor was December 12th 2006 by Ross Reinhold. This inventory identifies eight main types. Taken from the statement introducing the inventory, the question regarding personality type may be more accurately asked is: "Am I this way because I learned it or is this just the way I am?" This begs the question: Are we who we are as a consequence of our genetics or in response to the influences to which we have been exposed. This historic question of nature versus nurture is a tough one to answer as both influence our personalities and actions and what we recognize when we listen – who we are.

A third personality inventory is known as the David Keirsey type-temperament indicator. This instrument allows for the evaluation of the various aspects of the individual through which (s)he listens and is an aid in recognizing that listening is not a science but an art.

These inventories demonstrate the care with which individuals must evaluate listening. Within one culture there are a multitude of listenings. Consider the number of listenings and recognitions when that basic number is multiplied by ten or more cultures.

The authors of the inventories disagree with respect to the best method to use for personality discernment. Even within companies revisions continue to be made. Such an example is the resource designed along the perspectives of Carl Jung & Isabel Briggs Myers and their typological approach to personality -- Jung Typology Test™ 2010 at Humanmetrics. com. As things continue to evolve, who is to say whether the result is greater understanding?

Audition: the act of hearing

The complexities of listening by other animals have not been researched to the extent of that of humans. But listening, at least on the functional auditory level, has been observed, even by you.

Listening by humans may be compared to that accomplished by another mammalian species, dogs:

> Consider – the dogs in the neighborhood are howling. They appear to be attempting to cover their ears and to be in pain. A short time later you hear the police siren. What just happened?

Dogs listen with different pitch discernment than that of humans. It took a little time before the siren sound was in the range of human hearing. Another manner in which dog listening has been found to be different is in the dogs' trained ability to sniff out drugs in travelers' luggage. It is now recognized that some species of dog can tell when a person as about to have a seizure thirty minutes before the event.

The pitch of sound is based on the level of tension placed on the membranes of the inner ear. At the rear of the inner ear is found the nerve system which carries the messages to the brain where they are interpreted for our listening pleasure.

In the case of the human voice, wind from the lungs causing the vibration of the vocal cords, is picked up by the ear and hearing, discussed previously, occurs. Listening, therefore, is a mixture of external to internal and internal to external events.

Note that our recognition of the vibrating or change in wave lengths as sound varies. The farther away one is from a sound source (the vibrating object) the softer the sound. Consider sound as a point, the sound source. The sound radiates in a spherical fashion from this original point. The surface area of the sphere becomes larger and, because the sound source is assumed to be of constant intensity and the area is increasing, the sound intensity must be decreasing as the distance between the end point and the sound source increases. Stated differently, sound intensity is inversely proportional to distance from the sound source, squared. This is the inverse square law.

Sound moves through air from its vibrating source to a receiving object causing the receiving object to begin vibrating. This vibrating object, in turn, causes a movement of air molecules that corresponds to the vibration of the object. The wavelength of vibration is a measure of the distance between successive pressure points in the sound wave.

Listening as a function of the ear and the brain is an exciting concept. Truly! The interaction of air currents and nerve fibers is effected through conversion action. The liquid found in the ear system is excited such that the sound frequencies are separated and transmitted to the brain thus allowing the human to 'hear'.

For a complete and detailed description of hearing and sound you may consult one of the references at the end of this book dealing with the ear and hearing. Listening is exciting and more extensive than the scope of the concept as developed here. One last word has to do with the cilia (hair-like projections) that are an important part of listening.

Have you ever seen a one-hinged gate being blown by the wind? That picture describes, simply, the mechanism that allows listening to result in hearing. As the vibrations pass over the cilia they bend or twist depending on how solidly they are hinged to their link point. There are thousands of them and the combinations of positions and oscillations and acoustic pressures effect the glorious dimensions to sound which allow humans to distinguish between a robin and a crow, a mouse and a weasel, a spring breeze and a tornado, etcetera.

Chapter Five – Listening and our Other Senses

Listening with the other senses is equal in importance to that accomplished by the ear. While listening is generally thought of as an auditory function, the reality is that all the senses play an integral role to effective listening. These others 'listenings' are recognized by unique terms based on which of the five senses is doing that listening, which sensory receptors.

Listening accomplished with the nose

To discuss listening with the nose, it is important to understand the connection between the nose and the ear. The middle ear cavity is connected to the naso-pharynx (nose cavity and nose) by the Eustachian tube. Listening accomplished through the ears is joined by the sense of smell, a very important and long lasting listening mechanism.

The human nose contains a protective membrane known as the olfactory epithelium. Imbedded in this membrane is maze of thousands of receptor neurons designed to protect the body from harmful things that could enter through the nose. It also allows for the recognition and admission of those substances, oxygen for example, necessary for continuation of life. The nose and sense of smell is also connected to the mechanics of the mouth. The upper palate is the partition between the mouth and nose. As a result the senses of taste and smell mesh into one sensation.

Odorants that may be harmful to the body are disallowed by way of more shallow breathing, sneezing and flushing. Further away from the external orifice, inflammation and swelling may occur.

Odorants with favorable prior responses to them often produce acceptance behaviors. Loved ones long gone are brought to mind through their fragrances. The deceased loved one may come to mind when a scent is recognized on clothing worn or on blankets or household items. The memory of them sometimes even comes when we catch a whiff of the fragrance of their cologne or aftershave worn by someone else. The unfortunate thing about odorants is that there is no clean means of discerning good chemicals from the bad ones tagging along or of separating the bad from the good. Carbon monoxide, an odorless gas is very toxic, but unrecognizable by human listening technique of smell. Further, addictive behaviors may allow harmful odorants or pheromones to enter freely.

The term 'pheromones' is the scientific classification of the scent layperson simply recognizes as the 'way some memories are identified' of how something smells or tastes. Further, one such collection of odorants or pheromones are emitted by humans to assure the continuation of the species. The species has evolved to the point that such sexual signals, while recognized, may not be acted upon due to sociological norms. The bodies, however, continue to emit these reproduction demanding pheromones.

The expressions of the senses are collected, through neuron-impulses, and stored; all those sights, sounds, feelings, smells and tastes; in the short- and long-term memories in the brain. When re-experienced, the impulses are recognized as a duplicate. The original is recalled for your viewing and possible editing. The fragrance of a good friend is recognized as a pleasant impulse. Should that friend become an enemy editing occurs and the fragrance conjures up a different 'listening' expression.

The mucosa, the surface of the nasal cavity, secretes a thick fluid, a mixture of water and glycoprotein, commonly known as mucous. This mucous attaches to the chemicals when they are inhaled thus allowing for their dissolution as they enter the body through the nose. The dissolved chemicals are recognized by nerve cells in a fashion just like the process in the ear and forwarded to the brain. Cilia, receptor cells, olfactory nerve cells, brain. The process and the path are pretty basic. That we have learned to recognize tens of thousands of smells is a tribute to Homo sapiens' attention to detain. We listen.

Two main chemosensory modalities are olfaction, just discussed in regard to listening with the nose, and gestation which will be viewed next. The recognition functions accomplished by this duo has recently been named chemesthesis, and is defined as the listening effect of the chemical exchanges through the chemosensory modalities presented in both the nasal and oral orifices and interpreted in the brain.

Taste – Chemo receptors

That the human anatomy separates the nose and mouth by a thin palate is not coincidental. Both senses are used in the consumption of food. That juicy steak tastes and smells delicious! The salad smells, tastes, and sounds (hearing also, sometimes, comes into play) delectable or nasty, if it isn't to your memory store of things that you like. It may even be recognized as something spoiled or harmful to you.

Taste has to do with chemical as well as tactile experiences within the mouth. Specifically, by means of the tongue and the epithelial membranes within the oral cavity, substances are recognized and, with the aid of the saliva by the salivary glands to allow for the chemicals of which the food is composed to attach and be transported to the nervous system and the other parts of the digestive tract. There digestive juices in the stomach and other excretions as necessary from other glands convert the food into forms usable for human body nourishment or for elimination.

Let's look once again at the mouth, the muscular organ known as the tongue effects, along with teeth, the mastication, chewing, of food. The tongue turns that mouthful of stuff over and around such that the teeth are able to grind and press the pieces and mix the mass with saliva into a form able to be swallowed. That form is a breaking into more elemental chemicals of which food is composed and into a form the body can recognize, smell and taste, prior to the digestion process. The smell of food occurs before being placed in the mouth and by way of the connecting palate. Taste is chemical recognition by taste buds and epithelial cells. The chemical signals are forwarded to the dermis and the neurons beneath and the transfer continues, as in other listening systems, to the brain.

The basic tastes: sweet, sour, salty, and bitter; are recognized by different parts of the tongue. Collectively, they represent a set of receptor cells. The mechanical and thermal qualities of the substances are recognized by the frontal portion of the tongue. Cilia on the external end of each bud, just as with cells from the other senses, send messages to the brain. Short- and long-term memories tell us what we are consuming and whether or not we like.

Within the various parts of the body, other chemical signals are recognized and cause changes in cellular composition or other activity. An example is the non-diabetic body's ability to metabolize simple or complex sugars effectively as opposed to the diabetics' inability to do. Molecular recognition and expression goes through the central nervous system, the channeling system for all listening. This is an internal system operation that is connected directly to the mouth in ideal situations or through chemical injection into tissue, when necessary.

The body of man is pretty amazing. When listened to, it can tell you a lot.

Sight and Photoreceptors

The eyes are 'listened to'. We avoid obstacles that could injure us, find food, and move from place to place. Light is necessary for sight.

The truth is that the eyes are taught to do the avoidance and seeking tasks, as other listening instruments, by repetition. With the coordination of other senses and early training with those humans who are more proficient with the task the listening of sight is accomplished very well for the sighted individuals. Not all Homo sapiens have the luxury of sight, however. When this is the case, other signals must be relied on or the eyes of other mammals make take on this responsibility. When eyes are functional they sometimes need enhancement but always need light and connection to the nervous system.

You see the wind blowing by the effect it has on the branches of the trees, the dust and debris from the ground now competing for space in the atmosphere. Eyes are useful tools through which to see. In order to understand what is really going on when one says 'see' it is helpful to know the organ known as the eye.

The parts of the eye are the retina, the lens, the iris and pupil, and the cornea. Connected to the eye, at the rear, is the optic nerve. The retina is composed of rods and cones that interpret the light by way of their photoreceptor proteins. In addition the cones have pigment that allows for the discernment of color. Due to the fact that photoreceptor cells are more densely massed in the retina's center than at its periphery, one sees with greater clarity to something viewed directly.

Light received into the eye is converted to electrical impulses and transmitted, by way of the optic nerve, to the visual cortex of the brain. Once the message has reached the brain, the impulses are interpreted by the various layers of brain cells so that in a split-second one 'sees'.

Do you remember the delicious steak and the delectable salad? Before you tasted it, you saw it. Sight helped initiate the salivation process. Memory connected sight, smell and taste.

All those sounds, smells, sights, feels, and tastes are recognized through the functioning of neuro-transmitters and relayed to the brain where they are stored in the short- and long-term memories. Their retrieval, through conscious or unconscious effort, is what it means to listen.

Mechanoreceptors of touch, sound, and pressure

If you take just a moment to look back at the descriptions of hearing and seeing, perhaps you will recognize the listening through 'feel' imbedded within each of them. Skin, the largest human organ, without much fanfare accomplishes the task of augmenting the listening accomplished through other senses. Further, through its tactile sense, the skin calmly, quietly, and effectively watches out for the well-being of the entire body. The skin responds to temperature variances, external and internal, to protect the human body from gross abuse and alerts the mind/ nervous system of a probable need for more extensive attention that is accomplished by the individual or acquired through the assistance of medical professionals with their more knowledgeable listening efforts.

The existence of thermo receptors is very apparent when in conditions of temperature extremes. When it is hot most humans sweat and when it is cold most humans shiver. These recognizable effects of the temperature are an attempt by the body to maintain normal temperature. Perspiration evaporates and cools the skin, while shivering is an attempt by the body to raise the temperature.

In the case of illness high fevers are accompanied by perspiration which would effect the lowering of the body temperature. Unfortunately, the cause of the elevated temperature is the attempt on the part of the body to respond to what it has seen – the invasion by pathogens has occurred and the body is fighting to kill them. Therefore the body is getting mixed signals and isn't sure which message needs to be followed.

The wind of the thunderstorm scenario, found later in this book, alerts the tactile listening mechanism, by way of pressure. The nerves imbedded in the skin say 'watch out! It may be time to go inside or, at the very least, put on a jacket.'

Sight, hearing, and feeling represent avenues through which Homo sapiens exist compatibly, within the cosmos. Collectively they say 'LISTEN.'

Chemical Recognition again

Taken from a study [Bryant and Silver], Chemical recognition may be seen as a subset of the thermo-receptors. The tongue, when sensitized by a specific chemical will respond with an increase in the heat and pain responses. Repeated sensitization may result in the avoidance behavior or in desensitization, and with it, the lowering of levels of heat and pain, and the initiation of enjoyment. The common 'test' is the use of mind to hot peppers and the decreased sensitivity to same. Another response is the increased secretion of mucous in the mouth, eyes, and nasal area.

Odor for attracting mates has been studied in lower forms of life and in humans. Ants, moths, goldfish as well as snakes, mice, and others have shown this method of attraction to be true. Female Homo sapiens emit odorants, pheromones, to attract the opposite gender for the purpose of reproduction. The substance is produced by the female, when ovulation is present, and is received by the male, who then may respond by intercourse to join the sperm with the egg. One study suggests this odor emission by females affects other females with respect to their ovulation cycle [Bonner] but more study is warranted before anything of a conclusive nature can be stated.

> As I was walking one autumn day, I unexpectedly had a memory of my youth. Youth was, for me, a happy time, but I hadn't remembered it for decades. Why did this memory resurface in a time and place so distant from the original event? I stopped, closed my eyes, inhaled, and I knew. It was an odorant. I looked around and saw poplar

leaves which had fallen from a Poplar tree – the type of tree that used to line each side of the street where I lived and played. It was another time and place, but the odorant attached to those pleasant memories is stored in my long-term memory. With the trigger, the odorant from the leaves, allowed those memories to flood into my present day experience.

Listening as an internal body event or The Internal Body and What it means to Listen

The heart and the other parts of the circulatory system; lungs and other parts of the respiratory system; the stomach and other parts of the digestive system; plus the skeletal system and other internal parts of the body work as a unit to keep us alive. Each part has a dependency and a responsibility. This listening is intense and cannot be understated. The scope of this discussion, however, does not allow for the detailed explanations of all of these physical and chemical mechanisms. One important note is that they depend on the nervous system as much as do the external listenings and we would be lost without them. Diabetes has already been discussed as an internal listening and a few other internal listenings will be discussed, though not in great detail.

Pain receptors, nociceptors, are found throughout the body, externally and internally. They are nerve endings which respond to pain and signal the release of chemicals called prostaglandins. Therefore, when one indicates (s)he has 'felt' something, really what is meant is that an event has caused the initiation of secretion of chemicals that is interpreted by the brain as 'feel'. Prostaglandins cause such responses as inflammation and swelling in situations as a minor cut to a bronchial allergen. The body is listening when you put your foot in a hot tub of water, when you are stung by a bee, and when you eat something to which you are allergic. The body works hard and continuously to keep itself in a homeostatic state of wellbeing.

Osmoreceptors – osmotic pressure

A similar attempt by the body to effectively listen to its environments is through osmosis-receptors. These receptors sense change in osmotic pressure in internal systems such as in the blood and in urine. If a person drinks too much (or too little) water, the blood concentration level becomes too high or low, in relation to the body as a whole. To modulate that state, signals are received by the hypothalamus and action is taken to correct the situation.

Cells that are sensitive to changes in solute concentration of the blood, a group of osmosis-receptors are found in the hypothalamus, a small organ in the back part of the skull. From there these cells, through listening neurologic signals monitor changes in the osmotic pressure of the blood. When blood plasma level is too low or too high, plasma flows out of or into the blood through expansion or contraction of the vascular walls. When foreign chemicals exist, similar actions occur such that they are expelled. The normal kidneys function similarly through the use of this body listening tool. Mechanical dialysis becomes necessary when this listening process becomes defective.

Other osmosis-receptors are found in circum-ventricular system of the brain from where the hormone secretion or neurotransmission is initiated. Collectively these sites monitor the internal and external environments, responding to what is heard/ sensed to adjust the body in order to maintain chemical and fluid balance of the organism. The body is constantly being listened to.

Consider: two men are standing outside on a warm and sunny autumn day. One man is sweating profusely while the other man is not sweating. Beside differences in metabolism, one man may be wearing a winter coat while the other is in swimwear. Without all the information it is difficult to explain the two, different, conditions. That is the beauty of the body when it functions properly – it listens and reacts to all of the needed information.

Terms for listening change with the device used to achieve that listening. The concepts of 'listening' or what it means to listen unfold as the biological, emotional, cultural, and cosmos of which it is composed are explained and based on how the pieces fit together to make listening possible. The fifth component that flows through listening concept is wealth; but that component will not be discussed to any great extent in this book.

Bodies, along with their various and varied parts, exist in a continually changing state. So, too, the environment is constantly changing.

Consider: There is a glass filled with water. Next, three pieces of ice are placed in the water. After a period of time, the ice is no longer visible and there is water on the outer surface of the glass.

The condition of balance, homeostasis, is sought both inside and outside the glass. The ice inside the glass warmed to accommodate the temperature of the water and, similarly the water cooled to accommodate the temperature of the ice. Outside of the glass, the air cooled to accommodate the temperature of the glass and in the cooling process released some of its moisture. Similarly the glass warmed to accommodate the air. This demonstrated a complex series of listenings.

Listen to the Rain

Rain and specifically a thunderstorm is an excellent resource for a discussion about listening. There are many components to a thunderstorm and we have all experienced them. How do you listen to the rainfall? What are the processes through which you listen to a thunderstorm? Consider that you are sitting in a safe space, but one in which you may have all of the experiences surrounding a thunderstorm. What is going on with and to you? While this is not your first exposure, that first thunderstorm, with all the listening that occurred, remains vividly within you.

Clouds are entities seeking homeostasis. What happened in the two parts of the 'consider', above, is comparable to clouds and to the impending, ensuing, and ending aspects of a thunder storm. This storm is named because of its unique characteristic of producing thunder, a sound that does not occur in other types of rain fall, but what actually happens in a thunderstorm?

Listening to the Thunder Storm

With the sun's uneven heating of the earth and its atmosphere, thunderstorms are energized by the effects of the sun. As the sun heats the air in one area this causes an uneven pressure, thereby, allowing or causing the warm, lighter air to rise and leave a void in its wake. This void is then filled by heavier air in the vicinity. The updraft places the warm air in cooler air and the equalization of the multiple air temperatures causes two things: vertical currents and the release of water vapor, now water, into the volatile air mass we call a cloud.

Strong winds cause the water and colder ice crystals to bump up against each other. The rising water becomes charged while the falling moisture, still in the cloud, is oppositely charged. With the attraction of the oppositely charged entities comes the release of energy point, wherein the air between the two charges breaks down (becomes ionized to allow the currents to pass through) and a circuit is formed. The circuit discharges energy, heat, and light – lightning is what is seen and thunder is what is heard by this discharge of energy.

Lightning forms in five directions: (1) as energy flows within the cloud, (2) as flows of energy between clouds, (3) as energy flows from clouds to the air, (4) as cloud to ground lightning, and, most often, (5) as ground to cloud energy transfers. A flash of lightning actually consists of several discharges called 'leaders' and 'strokes'. "As the first spark moves from one location toward the next, it moves in a series of short bursts or steps with tiny pauses in between. As the bursts near the end point, another leader proceeds,

44

from the opposite direction, to meet it. The two join to make a channel through which electricity flows. The first discharge is immediately followed by a very bright, reverse direction-moving spark called the return stroke. The return stroke produces the light that we call lightning." [Green] These multiple events are what are seen as one long flash. Whether it is within or outside the cloud, what we see is an amazing light-show.

Dr. Thelma Bowles

Thunder

The current, or flow, of electrical charge within each lightning discharge is equal to twenty million volts, or as much light as 100 million light bulbs. "Lightning also creates heat that is about five times greater than that of the sun. This intense heat turns the air around the lightning into a gas called plasma, which reaches about 18,000° F. The plasma's heat causes the air around it to expand with great force and speed, disturbing the surrounding atmosphere with a series of high-pressure waves. This disturbance causes the booming sound of thunder." [Netzley]

Moisture Descending upon the Earth

The forming of thunder clouds begins with masses of hot air. Air became warm and then hot as a consequence of being heated, by the sun and/ or ground surfaces. Warm air is lighter than cool air and, thus, the warmer air rises into and through the cooler air. These combinations of warm and cool air are recognized as clouds, first white and then gray to black as the amount of condensed water vapor increases and small droplets of water (rain) increase in size. Note: the warm and cool airs may become mixed by the simple raising of the former to the level of the simple 'swishing together' by wind currents, rarely moving at the same speed. The method by which the varied temperature air comes together doesn't matter. The result is the same: the air temperatures equalize and water vapor becomes water, or, in some cases frozen water, what is called sleet or hail depending on the size of the individual pellets, or snow. At the point where the upward moving warm air can no longer hold the materials, the substances; rain, sleet, hail, or snow; fall to the ground as precipitation pulling some of the lower air with it.

Three types of Clouds

The three types of clouds affect the earth differently. The Cirrus Clouds, because they are so high above the earth, release water vapor in the icy form. Due to the altitude, this precipitation dissipates before touching the earth. The Cumulus Clouds are at altitudes too low to produce rain. The cumulous cloud can grow into the cumulonimbus or thunder clouds by rising in altitude and producing more rain particles, or by being in the presence of more cold air. The Cumulonimbus or thunder Clouds are the clouds which effect thunder storms or, at lower temperatures, sleet or snow storms.

Chapter Six – Sociology and Listening

In the beginning was the gene. This statement is, obvious, to most of you, as the paraphrased use of the pronouncement in the opening line of the Bible (Genesis 1:1) to the establishment of the cosmos by the creator. The wonder and fascination of fairy tales may draw from the similar inauspicious beginning. 'Once upon a time, there was …
.' Both literary types have held and captured the minds and dreams for a perfect existence from the beginning of recognized time. Again, 'In the beginning was the gene.'

Each individual is a collection of genes, which have evolved through the centuries. The evolution began with the two (2^1) nearest ancestors, the mother and father. Before that were the next closest ancestors, there were four (2^2) of them, known as grandparents. The tract continued backward into the eons, all the way to 2^∞. This suggests, nay concludes, each individual is composed of many varied genetic structures. In addition to that many biological iterations, in the same fashion, individual Homo sapiens are a conglomeration of

2^∞ sociologies, at least. With this in mind, consider listening as a sociological construction.

Mammals exist in societies. The characteristics of those societies vary by species and the nature of the interior and exterior cultures in which they manage their existence. Homo sapiens are part of the mammalian society, but so too are horses and cats. The interior culture, including the biological makeup, of each of these three societies consists of many opportunities to listen both within and among those unique societies.

The symbiotic relationship of the succeeding generation within the body of the female of the present generation is the initial listening to which the being is subjected. At birth the infants have varying degrees of innate abilities to exist with the environments and on their own as a consequence of their species.

The Horse as a Social Being

Horses live in bands and as such are considered social animals. This assumes they have control of their existence and are not controlled by Homo sapiens. The band is composed of the stallions, mares, and offspring. The control is given to the female who is responsible for finding foliage and water, critical for the existence of the family. With respect to reproduction, nature has determined the mare will ovulate in a twenty-one day cycle. The impregnation rights go to the stallion able to fend off other candidates.

Gestation is approximately 34- days and results in one foal. Horses are precocious, being able to stand and run minutes after birth. This is a good thing due to the nomadic existence and danger from predators to which the herd is routinely exposed.

In addition, horses are able to sleep in an upright position and do so in multiple short periods of time, always alert to the possible need to evade their enemies. To address the enemy situation, multi-stallion herds do exist. The additional stallions provide added fighting power and protection for the entire herd.

When in non-threatening environments, the young are allowed to play. This activity is a socialization mechanism and centers around different activities based on gender. Colts fight while fillies preen.

Dr. Thelma Bowles

Feline existence and societal listening

The feline category of mammal ranges from our domesticated cats through the self-sufficient and 'wilder' cousins categories such as lions and cougars. The basic feline social unit consists of the female and her kittens. After kittens are weaned, females of the litter may stay with the group as an extended family of caregivers. Young males more often leave or are forced away by a dominant older male participant in the group.

Females have the responsibility for foraging. The tom/ male cats protect the integrity of the unit by preventing other males from inducing ovulation of the females or attempting to assume control of the harem.

Human Sociology

Homo sapiens and the impacts on themselves and other mammalian cultures, with respect to listening, have been developed and continue to develop as a consequence of socialization and the other interpersonal activities collectively addressed in the field of sociology. A small tip of that iceberg will be elucidated next, along with the request that you internalize the information and add your own take on society and interpersonal behavior as it pertains to you.

Homo sapiens require extensive nourishment and care as newborns and into infancy. This extended mother-child connection provides the senior members of species time to impact the offspring with social norms and fears by providing them with repeated opportunities to listen to what is deemed right/ acceptable and what is considered inappropriate, based on the specific culture in which they are placed. Recent data on the role of play suggests such behaviors may be best interpreted as learning how to make and recover from social mistakes. The social experiences learned through play in childhood are important tools for normal social interaction in the adult cultural setting.

Dr. Thelma Bowles

Human Sociology, Human Listening

The world population has become closer than it was even a half century ago. With technology bringing world problems into homes on a regular basis, global events occur in an apparent connectedness not previously apparent. This present time interaction that once took weeks of months to address has proven to be problematic with some human beings. Consequences sometimes are represented as the tendency toward fatalism and the desire to fulfill personal desires immediately rather than through an extended process of socialization. The study of societal overload with the corresponding justification of human behavior is considered next. Moral codes, needs versus wants, and rights of self and others are concepts that flow through the socialization listening.

Personal Rights and Responsibilities

Are you male and the first born of a twentieth century North American family of Anglo-Saxon origin? Do your views and economy correspond with those of the religious and political upper economic class? To some part of this description most individuals must respond 'No'. Conversely, to assorted parts of this description the answer is a resounding 'Yes!'

Individuals listen in response to physical traits, but also as a consequence of personal and social exposures. A select few of the multitude of sociological human traits will be presented individually. That presentation in this form artificially represents their impact on listening is unavoidable. As more and more traits are inserted, the multiple combinations of the individuals thus represented become more difficult to keep track. The scope and opportunity for further development of this concept will provide much clearer understandings as to the challenge of listening in a diverse society.

The sociological traits which will be discussed are: gender, birth order, ethnicity, educational achievement, and environmental consciousness. Notable exclusions include: religion, region or country of origin, family structure, and first language. While the discussions clearly represent a limited description of the sociology of listening, the impact on listening made by societal 'place' should become obvious.

Gender

"Congratulations!" It's a boy. The medical staff has just given the news you had been hoping for. Girls are so much trouble to raise, according to your parents, who had only sons.

The society of the United States provides equality for both genders. Sports programs in public schools must allow equally for students without regard to gender. The facts tell a different story. Major sports leagues, those providing the best exposure are male. Another tough situation has to do with education in the sciences. While very strong efforts are made by many sectors of the culture, the old idea that math and science is for males just will not die. Very few women choose to go into those fields. Computer science may be the category which will turn this tide toward greater equality of interest.

Fashion seems, conversely to be dominated by women on the front stage. Men have accepted the challenge to consider this as a viable occupation and still be taken seriously. Similarly females are entering such fields as mechanics and electricians in growing numbers. Finally, as women are firmly in the workplace, it is more accepted that men assume domestic roles considered strictly women's work in the past.

This is a tough one. Despite the facts that each gender has its value in society and each has its strengths and weaknesses, the structure that is recognized continues to dominate places value, by place and money, on gender. Too much prior listening comes into play when the discussion of gender ensues. Suffice it to say, the United States societies have firmly entrenched places for each of the two genders.

Sociology and birth order

There are many psychology books that deal with birth order and whether there is an impact on the development of a person as a consequence of placement in birth order. While an argument can be made in either direction, there is disagreement among the 'experts'. The following is a snippet of what an infant may hear soon after birth. There are continual comparisons, actual or implied, throughout one's life. Those comparisons are sometimes vocalized by the individuals themselves. The question becomes, is it fact or self fulfilling 'prophecy', or does the nature versus nurture conflict enter this conversation?

What was your placement with respect to birth among four siblings? Were you the baby, forever and always? Perhaps you were the dreaded *middle* child. Or perhaps you had the good fortune to be the prima donna first born (with all the rights and responsibility that continues to this day). Did my statements strike a nerve? Do you have any biases as a consequence of prior listening?

Does how you listen really have anything to do with birth place? Let us consider the messages you received, and internalized for later use, as a consequence of where in the familial scheme of things, you were born.

Consider:

You are the firstborn and you hear your parents being told that as new parents they must take more adult responsibility. Further they must take fewer trips and save their money to assure their child, you, has a good college education.

Perhaps you, as the infant, hear: "Oh isn't he (she) cute/ handsome? (S)he looks just like (some respected family member). A great career is in his/ her future."

The whole family planned and attended the baby shower. It was great and the things 'mom' received for the new baby were fantastic! Someone may have given you a taste of ice cream while cooing over you.

When another child arrives, the firstborn may now hear: (First born) will now have someone to play with/help care for. You've been listening, so what have you internalized. It is not that these types of comments come only in the early years; our society seems to keep on making these types of statements which are rarely proven to be wrong.

What if you are the second born? What type of early chatter are you likely to hear. To what do you listen?

"(S)he will look perfect in (firstborn)'s little outfits." "(S)he looks just like (firstborn)."

The baby shower was smaller this time. Some of the friends and family couldn't come, but many of them sent gift cards. There was no ice cream from that cooing adult, she was in a retirement home and too sick to attend.

Though you didn't hear it, there was the undercurrent of 'Can they handle two in this slow economy? Or 'That's great! Their children are going to be so smart because the parents are and two children being raised together is a very good thing.'

Baby (last born):

There was no baby shower. The party with its gaiety didn't happen. There were no hugs and kisses. The house was more cluttered, less clean and older. You 'make do' with lots of 'hand-me-downs'. There may be parental arguing or an absent father.

The contrary tone may be that at last we have a child of the other gender. We are so excited and have great plans for him/her.

These statements and scenarios do not mean the child, turned adult, will be great or horrible. They do reflect impacts on one's life and are just one snapshot of what a person hears, feels, tastes, smells, and feels as a result of birth order. Those 'listenings' may be positive, negative, or neutral. They do exist.

Dr. Thelma Bowles

Ethnicity

Much study has been made of individuals of diverse ethnicities. The interactions of cultures and their success to 'failure' ratios have said there is little difference based simply on ethnicity when it comes to child to adulthood success. Why, then, if this is true, do cultures differ in such things as discipline, the place of aged members in the hierarchy of the group, the value placed on formal education, and the list goes on. What is seen to be highest in value, based on ethnicity?

When different ethnic cultures are compared, one similarity is that the cultures have evolved away from the extended family unit, values have changed. Place of possessions, religion, self and personal rights in their system of what is valued rate more highly than the continuum of life. The strong survive and the rights belong to the strong is a concept which is losing ground with respect to being a valued statement. Without regard to the ability of a particular group to fend for themselves, the society makes sure proper advocacy is forth coming.

With the evolution into a world environment and regular mixing of people with different ethnicities the reality is that ethnicity is evolving into a non-factor when listening to what impacts individuals as participants in the world experience.

Sociology and Education in relation to listening

Primary public education in America is funded through taxes and relies on parental involvement in the learning process for the greatest hope for student motivation and student success. This parental involvement varies as a consequence of the ability of the parents to allocate time for their child(ren) in this area. While not always the case, educational level of parents and grandparents is often seen as having a moderating impact of how well the child learns.

While this statement if not true for all situations, children residing in the more affluent areas of a community, generally, have more diverse and concentrated experiences for overall human development. This in many cases results in opportunities for more esteemed positions in society in the future. Parental involvement may be good or bad as a consequence of the human values learned by the parents in their evolution to adulthood.

Less affluent areas which consist of adults just trying to 'make ends meet' and who have not heard the message that a structured learning environment is critical for their children's future success may allow 'the system' to make decisions for educating their children. The results are often, although not always, the continuation of hard financial times and marginalization in the society for future generations.

The children for whom education is seen as a priority for them and as preparation for their future place in society, listen to this message and internalize it. Their behavior and self imposed structure reflect this listening. The boundary testing and acting out type cries for help and/or attention are not generally as extreme so as to cause physical or psychological harm to themselves or to others or to result in permanent exclusion from the main social environment.

A downside of our present learning is that the media and the mindset of buying and having more things are equated as good, have resulted in a listening behavior which may contaminate the moral existence. Have, at any cost, often leads to sacrificing the good of the many for the wants of the few. A clear example of this is the world population with many countries having to deal with diseases which had been nearly eradicated. Are we listening? Those in power sometimes forget why the power is in their hands. But the powerful are not totally to blame as indifference on the part of the masses allows for the corruption of power. John Acton, historian and moralist, expressed the opinion in 1887 that "Power tends to corrupt, and absolute power corrupts absolutely. Great men are almost always bad men." While the last sentence is not without controversy, the first part seems to be true. Continued vigilance on the part of the masses to listen and respond to the actions of those chosen to lead us is critical. They must be held accountable and challenged to continue to act honorably.

Intelligence versus time on task – Are we listening?

Was anything stated about the intelligence of the children in the above two situations? No. The truth about intelligence is that it is not known what it is. What does seem to be clear is that structure is the desirable condition for most children. The limit testing on the part of children begins in infancy and continues through adolescence. It is an attempt to identify the nature of the structure in which they are to live. Assuming no medical reason to the contrary, time on task determines the success of an experience.

Blowing in the Wind – Gossip and Inaccurate Listening

Listening carries the hope that something of worth will be acquired. When a 'trigger', something previously internalized, occurs, the attachments to those memories, negative or positive, are activated. With negative past experiences, the 'Red Flag' is raised and the self protection mechanisms of listening become engaged. Listening becomes guarded. If additional negative prior experiences are activated, further listening is directed so as to validate the negative experiences. Contrarily, should positive past experiences become recognized in the present listening, those memories are used to validate the present listening experience.

It's All about Me

The person of note has just moved into a new home and he is not sure of his acceptance. Further, this villa has a driveway which has an attachment to that of the neighbor. They share a section leading to the street. After he has used the neighbor's section as a turnaround a couple of times, the neighbor begins leaving a car in the driveway so that turn around in that section is not possible. The person of note has to back down the drive to reach the street or back up the drive from the street to reach his garage. He is angry with the neighbor whom he has not met and assumes neighborhood is an unwelcoming one.

A few weeks after moving in to the neighborhood, a neighbor rings the person of note's door bell. He answers the summons to discover someone welcoming him to the neighborhood. He is told of the services provided and given a packet containing information about those services. Perhaps the community is not the negative one of past experiences, the person of note considers.

He takes the initiative. The person of note goes to introduce himself to the neighbors in the house with whom he shares a driveway. They do not invite him inside their home. Actually 'they' is a single older woman with limited comfort with the English language. She is pleasant and considerate, not the 'harsh person' the *mind* of the person of note has created. Upon leaving the encounter, he remembers the 'car in the driveway' that prevented him from making the turnaround was actually different cars on differing occasions. Now his 'past programming' recognizes the situation differently. Perhaps the neighbor has children coming to check on her periodically. They leave the car in the drive because they are not staying or the garage is occupied with the neighbor's vehicle. It's not always "all about me" the person of note realizes.

Listening and Anthropology

Social development and behavior of Homo sapiens is, has been presented, a complex mix of exposures. As a result of, or in spite of, those exposures human interaction has evolved. Those who remember lyrics by Oscar Hammerstein II in the 1949 film South Pacific, will recall a segment of love lost. Through initial and succeeding exchanges between the two individuals, love grew. There was a compatibility which appeared to be true love by each individual for the other. With one development, however, the love by one party was destroyed. Lessons learned in childhood, as a means of protection against possible harm, had been carried over into adulthood without rationality.

'Always' and 'never' are two words that should be stricken from use. Few if any situations or things fall into those categories. Despite that understanding the terms are used as a quick way of discerning what may be best in a situation, the reason for giving one person or group of people preference over another, etcetera. Consider human interactions as snippets. Quick judgments are made based on surface considerations. This is a dangerous way to interact when, for the most complete assessment, an in depth assessment is required before judgment can more accurately be made. Certainly there are times when quick judgment of the situation is made and action, based on that judgment, taken. A dark cloud overhead may be a good reason to take immediate cover or to make sure the umbrella is handy. That cloud may or may not mean rainfall is eminent, but history may have told you there is a ninety percent chance of rain.

OK, why risk getting wet when there is an easy means of preventing that drenching?

With human interactions, however, there are so many variables that a quick conclusion, generally, results in an error in judgment, the loss of the opportunity for a positive outcome, or great fun. "Most of the things people worry about do not happen." To live one's life based on the possibility of that remote happening is an unfortunate way to live. While many view the present interpersonal relational perspective as an improvement over former ways, with all their superstitions, prejudices, and errors; it may be more accurate to identify the present as the transformation of the old life for a new one with the same attitudes only in different forms. How unfortunate!

Discussion

The facts of listening are that they are immersed throughout myriad locations that appear appropriate in our attention to the detail of living. Perhaps it is more accurate to indicate, the multitude of locations exist as consequence of the importance listening holds to the drama we call living.

Where listening is identified by the nature of work, the sciences: Biology, Anthropology, Psychology, Sociology, and Ecology immediately come to mind. Business, Polity, Economy, and Religion are not far behind when the subject of listening comes up. Clearly, those who are listened to and those doing the listening, impact these processes through their accumulated message sending and receiving over time. It is not always clear, but the fact remains 'listening identities' are fluid, changing within and between as needs dictate.

After a brief introduction (one question) we will proceed to two listening scenarios: "What do you understand to be the circumstances embodying listening"? (your answer here)   . Assuming you gave an answer, let us proceed to two scenarios, fortified with said answer to the question.

Scenario One

What are your thoughts about these wars today? With the way things are going, I think the world will have peace by the end of the year and everything will be back to normal.

I agree. Things are moving along so smoothly on 'the ground' that the pull back will be a pullout before long and the governments will be able to work on their common agendas of economic prosperity, health, and the environment.

Do you really believe the various governments, with their collateral business interests, are going to allow the state of peace to continue for very long? Simmering unrest will just erupt in another impoverished sector or some natural disaster will afford some special interest group an excuse to have their point made; whether it is the need to reinforce the dikes, rid the area of the sinful man, or feed the hungry from our coffers.

Scenario Two

Let's go to the mall and check out the (you insert) for the afternoon and then have some lunch at (you insert.) I have some time before (you insert) and I really feel like taking a break.

That sounds like a great idea. Just give me a minute to (you insert) and we can do it.

The two conversations seem basic enough. What was your comfort level in the first scene? Did the first or the second scenario appear reality? As the views concerning listening from the 'experts' are summarized and analyzed herein there will be many opportunities to revisit these, and other, scenarios in view of their collective wisdoms and yours.

It is fair to state that the sources are not inclusive or exclusive by intent. The sources and my interpretations of their explanations and views are open to your and others' scrutiny and different interactions. Welcome to a small slice of the world of and through listening.

The practice of medicine may or may not be seen as a profession wherein listening to patients occurs. Many patients believe they are not being listened to by their physicians. That is, generally, an inaccurate assessment of outward physician behavior. Processing by the doctor but not recognized by the patient contributes this perception of 'not being listened to'. The doctor manner may be a behavior which is the result of an extensive stream of listening. Accurate communication of senses and perceptions need to be part of the patient-doctor listening experience and other situations as well.

Please note: listening, to listen, talking, hearing, and other connections of senses (internally and interpersonally) have routinely, collectively, been known as 'to listen' in human common- and professional- verbiage. That custom is continued here.

Listening has been identified in infants as yet unborn. This listening has been documented through research into connections between mother and child and the heart rate of the fetus in various situations. In addition, a two day old child is able to recognize her mother's odor, a very strong measure for communication, and makes that recognition known with a smile or by intensely watching her, even when other adults are present. Such behavior will, if reciprocated, continue. [Howard]

Communication

The forms of communication are a response to the various listening behaviors observed and successfully practiced. Giving advice to someone may actually interrupt or disrupt dialog. What is requested in the dialog from the first person may sound like a call for help. The reality may be that the call is for a sounding board, someone to listen to the concepts/ thoughts/ attempted approaches in order for the first person to evaluate the scope of the possibilities. Should the second person, in an effort to help or to demonstrate superiority, supply a solution, the result may not be in harmony with the needs of the first person when 'listening' was sought. This listening dyad requires the use of the listening mechanisms of all the senses of both of the listening participants in order to achieve listening effectiveness.

Dr. Thelma Bowles

Listening and Neurosis

When considering the multitude of listenings with which individuals must contend in the attempt to negotiate the many pathways of life, mental and physical health issues frequently interfere with the positive and effective pursuits called 'life. Ericksson, Freud, Fromm, and others in the fields of psychology, psychiatry and psychoanalysis had much to impart in the attempt to keep Homo sapiens uniform with regard to listening and living life consistent to the wholeness of society. Those medical fields where doctors have attempted and continue to attempt to keep us safe and sane are too numerous to mention by name, but include neurologists, internists, surgeons, and general medical practioners. While their efforts may sometimes seem futile, they continue to help us exist and inter-exist such that the communally effective listenings of body and mind, sociology and economy, polity and peace, and harmony of man may be approached.

Mental field:

In this broad field, the helpers enable those with need to become consistent. That consistence is in recognizing the origin of anxieties and in acquiring the positive ego such that they, those seeking help and working toward the 'right' plateau of life, may acquire the tools to do so.

Conclusion

Listening is a very exciting concept. When viewed, as it has been here, as the sum total of connections made by entities and their voluminous environments it becomes quite an amazing feat! Listening between and among mammals has been perfected to effect the best cohabitation possible. When boundaries are overstepped listening of the destructive nature reminds the species involved of the need to respect each other's domain. Such reminders exist within the species know as Homo sapiens. Wars and talk of wars cause the loss of many lives and the contamination of many environments to no permanent positive solutions. To our great loss, man has fought man from the beginning of time. While other species appear to be more tolerant within their species, they too, on occasion venture forth to listen differently, to their own detriment.

The fire engine siren, the siren on the police car; the furnace automatically turning on; awakening on the beach to a sunburn; seeing a pair of alligator leather shoes; Thanksgiving turkey baking in the oven; the soft feel of a baby's cheek; you name it. What listening is elicited? What does your brain tell you? What are the variables unique to you?

This small venture into the nature of listening has been the sum total of my interactions and study and of the efforts of others, scientific and non-scientific. Your listening has accomplished different, but equally respected, results. Collectively, the future listenings will be better and worse as well as more and less intense. There is one statement which cannot be denied – Listening Exists.

A Final Note

When I decided to write down my thoughts about listening and how we listen, I, naively, figured the book project could be completed in three months tops. As I began to delve into the subject, revisions to the original tenor of the treatise became necessary. Concepts not previously considered to be encompassed by this topic repeatedly surfaced and their subject relevance could not be denied.

In an attempt to be as honest as possible, my years of listening were augmented with scientific research and presumptive study of others. I hope the sum total has achieved the goal which was sought – to enhance your listening and what it means to listen.

About the Author

The nature of this book has been exposed as a prelude to your further exploration about listening, what it means to listen, and the truth or fallacies being circulated regarding what it means to listen. The nature of the author has, as yet, not been exposed. To listen to this book without at least a minimal knowledge of the perspective from which the author listens would be harmful to you, the reader. Your level of acceptance of this summary of knowledge about listening must be tempered with an understanding of the receptacle, the cauldron, by which that knowledge has been collected, mixed, and brewed.

The cauldron is me, the author. A mathematics, biology, and business educator, as well as, counselor by trade; I lived in rural Michigan USA for over thirty years. During that time, I helped my five daughters and my husband to identify who they were in this cosmopolitan society and 'infected' them with my liberal biases. Myself the product of overachievers, I was expected to be and did become an overachiever; albeit with a late blooming fascination for science fiction. I rarely listen to fictional television. I do, on occasion, allow sports to drone on as background noise while I do other things. I find it necessary to listen to news casts periodically, but have difficulty discerning fact from fiction.

Listen is what I do. To understand it has been my most recent passion. Have I been successful at acquiring that understanding? You may judge.

Resources

Books

Back, Les (2007) <u>The Art of Listening.</u> Oxford, UK: Berg Publishers

Barnet, Ann B., R. J. Barnet (1998) <u>The Youngest Minds: Parenting and Genes in the development of intellect and emotion</u>. New York, NY: Simon & Schuster

Becker, Ernest (1962) <u>The Birth and Death of Meaning: a Perspective in Psychiatry and Anthropology</u>. New York, NY: The Free Press of Glencoe

Berg, Paul (1992) <u>Dealing with Genes: the language of heredity</u>. Mill Valley, California: University Science Books; Blackwell Scientific Publications

Berne, Eric (1964) <u>Games People Play: the psychology of human relationships</u>. New York, NY: Watts

Bonner, John Tyler (2000) <u>First Signals: the evolution of multicellular development</u>. Princeton, New Jersey: Princeton University Press

Borror, Donald J. and White, Richard E. (1970) <u>A Field Guide to Insects</u>. New York, NY: Houghton Mifflin Company

Bossard, James and Boll, Eleanor (1948) <u>The Sociology of Child Development</u>. New York, NY: Harper and Row, publishers

Brazelton, T. Berry M.D. and Bertrand, G. Cramer M.D. (1990) <u>The Earliest Relationship</u>. Reading, Massachusetts: Addison-Wesley Publishing Company, Inc.

Briskin, Alan (2009) <u>The Power of Collective Wisdom and the Trap of Collective Folly</u>. San Francisco, CA: Berrett-Koehler Publishers

Brueggemann, Brenda Jo (1999) <u>Lend Me Your Ear: Rhetorical Constructions of Deafness</u>. Washington, D.C.: Gallauder University Press

Cavendish, Martin (2003) <u>Bees</u>. Tarrytown, NY: Benchmark Books

Coen, Enrico (1999) <u>The Art of Genes: how organisms make themselves</u>. New York, NY: Oxford University Press

Edelman, Marian Wright (1992) <u>The Measure of Our Success: A letter to my children and yours</u>. Boston, Massachusetts: Beacon Press.

Finger, Thomas E., Silver, Wayne L., and Restrepo, Diego, editors 2nd edition (2000) <u>The Neurobiology of taste and Smell</u>. New York, N.Y: Wiley-Liss

> <u>Chemesthesis: The Common Chemical Sense</u>. Bruce Bryant and Wayne L. Silver pp.73-100.

Cell Biology of Taste Epithelium. Thomas E. Finger and Sidney A. Simon pp. 287-314.

Fox, Robin (1994) The Challenge of Anthropology: Old Encounters and New Excursions. New Brunswick, N J: Transaction Publishers

Fromm, Erich (1994) The Art of Listening. New York, NY: Continuum

Gintis, Herbert (2009) The Bounds of Reason: game theory and the unification of the behavioral sciences. Princeton, NJ: Princeton University Press

Goffman, Erving (1967) Interaction Ritual Essays in face-to-face behavior. Chicago, IL: Aldine Publishing Company

Gray, Susan Heinrichs (2006) The Ears. Chanhassen, Minnesota: Child's World Publishing

Greco, Thomas H. Jr (2009) The End of Money and the Future of Civilization. White River Junction, VT: Chelsea Green Publishing

Green, Jen (2008) Thunderstorms. Chicago, IL: World Book, Incorporated

Habermas, Jurgen (1984) The Theory of Communicative Action, volume I: Reason and the Rationalization of the Society. Translated by Thomas McCarthy. Boston, Massachusetts: Beacon Press

Halsey, A. H., editor (1977) Heredity and Environment, first American edition. New York, NY: Free Press. Chapter 2 Natural Selection in Mankind, "Sociology, biology and population control" by T. G. Dobzhansky

Hochschild, Arlie Russell (1989) <u>The Second Shift: working parents and the revolution at home</u>. New York, NY: Viking Penguin

Howard, Emma (2008) <u>Baby and Toddler Body Language Phrasebook</u> . San Diego, California: Thunder Bay Press

Hughes, Howard C. (1999) <u>Sensory Exotica</u>. Cambridge, Massachusetts: The MIT Press

Karen, Robert (1977) <u>Becoming Attached</u>. New York, NY: Warner Brothers, a Time Warner Company

Keirsey, David & Bates, Marilyn (1984) <u>Please Understand Me: Character and Temperament Types</u>. Del Mar, CA: Prometheus Nemesis Book Company

Klug, William S. and Cummings, Michael R. (2005) <u>Essentials of Genetics,</u> fifth edition. Upper Saddle River, New Jersey: Pearson Prentice Hall

Mezzanotte, Jim (2007) <u>Thunderstorms</u>. Milwaukee, Wisconsin: Weekly Reader Early Learning Library

Møller, Aage R. (2006) <u>Hearing; Anatomy, Physiology, and disorders of the auditory system</u>. Burlington, MA: Elsevier Academic Press

Mound, Laurence (1990) <u>Insects</u>. New York, NY: Alfred A. Knopf, Inc.

Netzley, Patricia D. (2003) <u>Thunderstorms</u>. Farmington Hills, MI: Kidhaven Press

Noble, David (1992) <u>A World Without Women: The Christian Clerical Culture of Western Science</u>. New York, NY: A.A. Knopf

Ramachander, S. (2006) <u>Creativity @ Work</u>. New Delhi, India: Response Books

Sherman, Josepha (2002) <u>The Ear: Learning how we hear</u>. New York, NY: Rosen Publishing Group, Incorporated

Simon, Seymour (2003) <u>Eyes and Ears</u>. New York, NY: Harper Collins Publishers

Smith, Adam (1793) <u>an Inquiry into the Nature and Causes of the Wealth of Nations</u>, the seventh edition. London, England: Printed for A. Strahan; and T. Cadell, in the Strand.

Speier, Matthew (1973) <u>How to Observe Face-to-face Communication: a Sociological Introduction</u>. Pacific Palisades, CA: Goodyear Publishing Company, Inc.

Thomson, Ruth (2010) <u>A Bee's Life Cycle</u>. New York, NY: Rosen Publishing Group

Wells, Herbert George (1922) <u>A Short History of the World</u>. New York, NY: Macmillan Company

Yost, William (2007) <u>Fundamentals of Hearing: an introduction 5th edition</u>. Burlington, MA: Elsevier Academic Press.

Journals and Presentations

Collins, F. S., & Mansoura, M. K. (1992). The Human Genome Project : Revealing the Shared Influence of all Humankind. *Cancer, Supplement*, 221-25.

DeCasper, A. J., Lecant, J., Busnel, M., Granier-Deferre, C., & Maugeais, R. (1994). Fetal Reactions to Recurrent Maternal Speech Infant Behavior & Development. *Journal of the American Medical Association*, 17: 159-164.

James, Charles J. (1982) Are You Listening? The Practical Components of Listening Comprehension. *Annual Meeting on the Teaching of Foreign Languages* Presented November 25-27.

Subramian, G., Adams, J. C., Venter, & Broder, S. (2001) Implications of the Human Genome for Understanding Human. Biology & Medicine. *Journal Occupational & Environmental Medicine*, 37: 91-99.

VanDame, K., L. Casteleyn, Heseltine, E., Huici, A., Sorsa, M., vanLarabeke, N., & Vinelis, P. (1995) Individual Susceptibility & Prevention of Occupational Disease: Scientific & Ethical Issues. *Journal Occupational & Environmental Medicine* 37: 91-99.

Myers-Briggs Personality Inventory© (2010) Gainesville, FL: CPP, Inc

Internet

www.answers.com

www.britannica.com

www.encyclopedia.com (2008) "Cro-Magnon man"

www.equisearch.com (2007) Pascoe, Elaine. "How Horses Sleep, Pt. 2 – Power Naps"

www.horsekeeping.com (2010) Bryant, Jennifer. Horse book: The **USDF Guide** to **Dressage**

www.horsetalk.co.nz (2007) Hanggi, Evelyn B. "Understanding horse intelligence"

www.humanmetrics.com (2010) Jung, Carl & Briggs Myers, Isabel. Jung Typology Test™ typological approach to personality.

www.medical-dictionary.thefreedictionary.com

www.merckvetmanual.com (2008) Whitehouse Station, NJ: Merck & Co., Inc.

www.personalitypathways.com Reinhold, Ross (2006) Cognitive Style Inventory©

www.phrases.org.uk

www.press.jhu.edu

www.wikipedia.com

www.wisegeek.com